HAPPY BI

TO

. . . .

WITH LOVE FROM

. . . .

And Jackie

HAPPY BIRTHDAY—LOVE . . .

Complete Series

Jane Austen

Joan Crawford

Bette Davis

Liam Gallagher

Audrey Hepburn

John Lennon

Bob Marley

Marilyn Monroe

Michelle Obama

Jackie Kennedy Onassis

Elvis Presley

Keith Richards

Frank Sinatra

Elizabeth Taylor

Oscar Wilde

HAPPY BIRTHDAY

Love, Jackie

ON YOUR SPECIAL DAY

ENJOY THE WIT AND WISDOM OF

JACQUELINE KENNEDY ONASSIS

FIRST LADY

Edited by Jade Riley

CELEBRATION BOOKS

THIS IS A CELEBRATION BOOK

Published by Celebration Books 2023
Celebration Books is an imprint of Dean Street Press

Text & Design Copyright © 2023 Celebration Books

Cover by DSP

ISBN 978 1 915393 70 8

www.deanstreetpress.co.uk

HAPPY BIRTHDAY—LOVE, JACKIE

THERE will never be, and never could be, another
Jacqueline Kennedy. She belonged to her age;
a time when debutantes wore long, white gowns
and attended balls in Newport, Rhode Island. When
giant yachts sailed briskly past elegant mansions and
private clubs were the norm. Finishing schools were
de riguer for society daughters. Jackie Kennedy was
born to this world. But she was a different kind of girl.
Certainly she adored her horses and her sports, but
books, art and culture were the loves of her life. Jackie
was brought up to marry a wealthy man and never
to work. But the strong-willed Jackie went to college,
and then found employment as a photo-reporter in

Washington D.C. She had already lived abroad as a student and studied five languages. She was an "It" girl who took life seriously. With a combination of beauty, intelligence and *savoir faire*, she became the role model and the image of American femininity.

As the youngest first lady of the United States, she and President John F. Kennedy captured the country's imagination. Upon finding the White House décor in shambles, she restored and bought back many of its original antiques by establishing a charitable committee to raise the funds. She would host marvelous artists and musicians at the White House. She even managed to persuade France to lend the *Mona Lisa* to American museums so local people could know the joys of the Leonardo da Vinci masterpiece.

Jackie Kennedy was grace under pressure and effortless elegance. She could entertain hundreds or simply preside over a family picnic. Whatever she did, she did it with the class of a bygone era coupled with the modernity of a working woman. Take up Jackie's words on Life and get inspired all over again.

Jacqueline Kennedy

Pearls are always appropriate.

A great goal in
life is the only
fortune worth
finding.

I am a
woman above
everything
else.

We should all do something to right the wrongs that we see and not just complain about them.

"If you cut people off from what nourishes them spiritually, something in them dies.

I am happiest
when I am
alone.

Americans care about their past, but for short-term gain they ignore it and tear down everything that matters.

One should
always dress
like a marble
column.

Stay loyal to
those who
love you.

You have to have been a Republican to know how good it is to be a Democrat.

"

You must
continue.

"

Poets are the ones who change the world.

If you produce one book, you will have done something wonderful in your life.

We are the only country in the world that trashes its old buildings. Too late we realize how very much we need them.

One man can
make a difference
and every man
should try.

I would rather
be a lucky rider
than a good
one.

I'll be a wife and mother first, then First Lady.

I don't think there
are any men who
are faithful to
their wives.

[On Hillary Rodham Clinton:] She's intrepid; she's the biggest bargain America ever got, bigger than that Louisiana Purchase from my French friends.

You have only
one chance
to raise your
child.

A camel makes an elephant feel like a jet plane.

It's much more fun
traveling in second or
third class and sitting up
all night in trains, as you
really get to know people
and their stories.

If you make your living in public office, you're the property of every tax-paying citizen. Your whole life is an open book.

"

One must not let oneself
be overwhelmed by
sadness.

Even though people may be well known they still hold in their hearts the emotions of a simple person for the moments that are the most important of those we know on earth—birth, marriage, death.

I think the best thing I can do is to be a distraction. A husband lives and breathes his work all day long. If he comes home to more table thumping, how can the poor man ever relax?

The only
routine with
me is no
routine at all.

A newspaper reported
I spend $30,000 a year
buying Paris clothes and
that women hate me for
it. I couldn't spend that
much unless I wore
sable underwear.

Sex is a bad thing because it rumples the clothes.

Never chew in public.

Being away from
home gave me
a chance to look
at myself with a
jaundiced eye.

March, young man.

I wish I knew when to breathe. I just don't know how actresses can do it.

Whenever I was upset by something in the papers, [Jack] always told me to be more tolerant, like a horse flicking away flies in the summer.

I think the major role of the
First Lady is to take care
of the President so that he
can best serve the people.
And not to fail her family,
her husband, and children.

Once you can express yourself, you can tell the world what you want from it. All the changes in the world, for good or evil, were first brought about by words.

Why are people
so interested in
what I wear and
how I fix my hair?

The one thing I do not want to be called is First Lady. It sounds like a saddle horse.

"Oh, Mr. Chairman, don't bore me with statistics.

An Editor becomes kind of your mother. You expect love and encouragement from an Editor.

I don't understand it. Jack
will spend any amount
of money to buy votes
but he balks at investing
a thousand dollars in a
beautiful painting.

[To Oleg Cassini:] Just make sure no one has exactly the same dress I do . . . I want all of mine to be original and no fat little woman hopping around in the same dress.

[On The White House:] It looked like it'd been furnished by discount stores.

Like everyone else,
I have to work my
way to an office
with a window.

A wonderful book is one that takes me on a journey into something I didn't know before.

If school days are the happiest days of your life, I'm hanging myself with my skip-rope tonight.

The trouble with me is that I'm an outsider. And that's a very hard thing to be in American life.

History—it's
what those
bitter old men
write.

Aristotle rescued me.

What can one say about Michael Jackson? He is one of the world's most acclaimed entertainers, an innovative and exciting songwriter whose dancing seems to defy gravity and has been heralded by the likes of Fred Astaire and Gene Kelly.

"The river of sludge will go on and on. It isn't about me.

"

I want to live
my life, not
record it.

It's really
frightening to lose
one's anonymity
at thirty-one.

Now, I think that I should have known that he was magic all along. I did know it—but I should have guessed that it would be too much to ask to grow old with and see our children grow up together. So now, he is a legend when he would have preferred to be a man.

There will be great
presidents again
but there will
never be another
Camelot.

"I want minimum information given with maximum politeness.

Our culture will become like it was during the medieval times when there truly was a cultural elite. The rest of the people will just watch television, which will be their only frame of reference.

Everything in the White House must have a reason for being there.

There are many little
ways to enlarge your
child's world. Love
of books is the best
of all.

The children have been a wonderful gift to me, and I'm thankful to have once again seen our world through their eyes. They restore my faith in the family's future.

What is sad for women of my generation is that they weren't supposed to work if they had families. What were they going to do when the children are grown— watch the raindrops coming down the window pane?

If you bungle raising your children, I don't think whatever else you do matters very much.

The first time you marry for love, the second for money, and the third for companionship.

You have to be
doing something
you enjoy. That
is a definition of
happiness!

If you want
things to be right,
you have to do
them yourself.

" You've got to marry up. "

Who me? Work?

There are two kinds of women: those who want power in the world and those who want power in bed.

" Being a
reporter seems
a ticket out into
the world.

When Harvard men say they have graduated from Radcliffe then we have made it.

Play a Rhumba next.

Would you rescue
a great artist who
is a scoundrel, or
a commonplace
family man?

I was a tomboy. I decided to learn to dance and then I became feminine.

I like men with funny noses, ears that protrude, irregular teeth, short men, skinny men, fat men. Above all he must have a keen mind.

I think my biggest
achievement is that,
after going through
a rather difficult time,
I consider myself
comparatively sane.

You are about to have your first experience with a Greek lunch. I will kill you if you pretend to like it.

Everyone should see Greece.

I'm always optimistic that people will buy good books.

A man
without a
child is
incomplete.

If the situation develops that requires the children and me to go to the shelter, let me tell you what you can expect. If the situation develops, I will take Caroline and John, and we will walk hand in hand out onto the south grounds. We will stand there like brave soldiers, and face the fate of every other American.

It's not as if
I've never
done anything
interesting.

One of the
chops fell on
the floor but I put
it on the plate
anyway.

Don't raise your kids
to have more than
you had, raise them
to be more than
you were.

The good, the bad, hardship, the joy, the tragedy, love, and happiness are all interwoven into one single, indescribable whole that is called life. You cannot separate the good from the bad. And perhaps there is no need to do so, either.

All I ask is someone with a little imagination, but they are hard to find.

I refuse to believe I am going to die.

Jacqueline Kennedy

ABOUT THE EDITOR

JADE Riley is a writer whose interests include old movies, art history, vintage fashion and books, books, books.

Her dream is to move to London, to write like Virginia Woolf, and to meet a man like Mr. Darcy, who owns a vacation home in Greece.

Made in United States
Orlando, FL
06 July 2023

34800007R00061